GUITAR | VOCAL

# JOHN PRINE
## GUITAR SONGBOOK

### 15 SONGS TRANSCRIBED IN STANDARD NOTATION & TAB

Music transcriptions by Pete Billmann

ISBN 978-1-5400-2197-7

Visit Hal Leonard Online at
**www.halleonard.com**

Contact Us:
**Hal Leonard**
7777 West Bluemound Road
Milwaukee, WI 53213
Email: info@halleonard.com

In Europe contact:
**Hal Leonard Europe Limited**
42 Wigmore Street
Marylebone, London, W1U 2RN
Email: info@halleonardeurope.com

In Australia contact:
**Hal Leonard Australia Pty. Ltd.**
4 Lentara Court
Cheltenham, Victoria, 3192 Australia
Email: info@halleonard.com.au

# CONTENTS

from *John Prine*

# Angels from Montgomery

**Words and Music by John Prine**

My old man ___ has a-noth-er child ___ that's grown ___ old. ___
He was-n't much to look at, just a free ram - blin' man. ___
And I ain't ___ done noth-in' since I woke up to-day. ___

If dreams ___ were light - 'ning, thun - der ___ were de - sire, ___
But that ___ was a long ___ time, and no mat - ter how I ___ try,
How the hell ___ can a per - son go to work ___ in the morn - in',

this old house ___ would-a burnt ___ down ___ a long ___ time a - go. ___
the years ___ just flow ___ by, like a brok - en down ___ dam.
and come home ___ in the ev - 'nin' and have noth-in' to say? ___

**Chorus**

Make me an an - gel ___ that flies from Mont-gom -'ry.

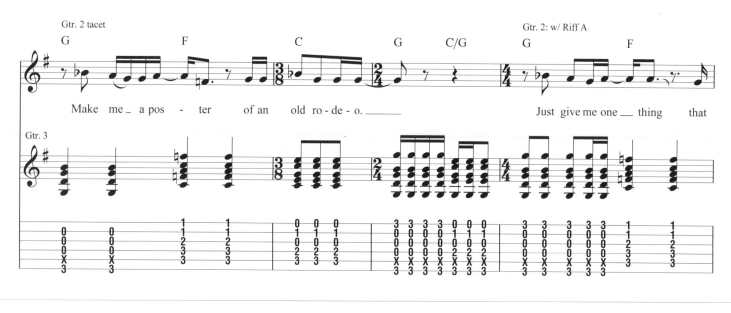

Make me a pos - ter of an old ro - de - o. _____ Just give me one _ thing that

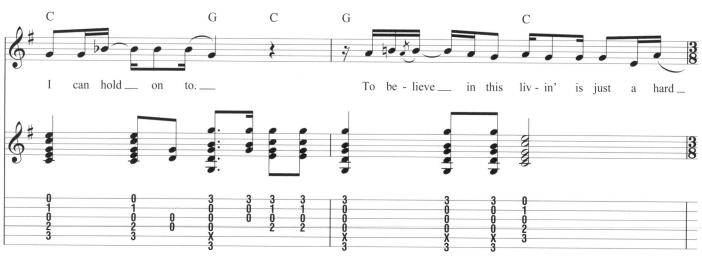

I can hold _ on to. _ To be - lieve _ in this liv - in' is just a hard _

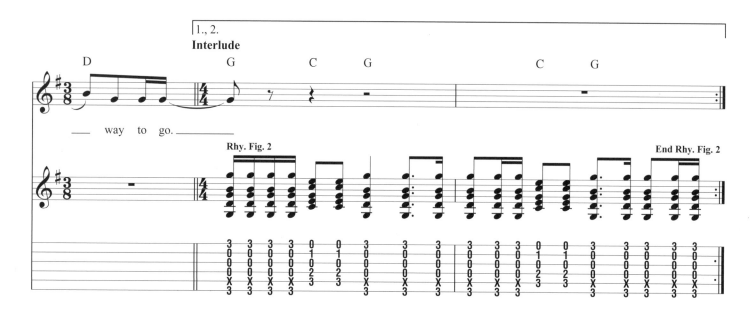

_ way to go. _____

from *Fair and Square*

# Clay Pigeons

## Words and Music by Michael Fuller

Capo III

**Intro**
Slow ♩ = 71

*Symbols in parentheses represent chord names respective to capoed guitar.
Symbols above reflect actual sounding chords. Capoed fret is "0" in tab.

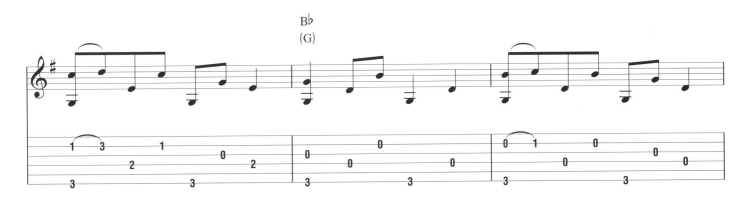

**T=Thumb on 6th string

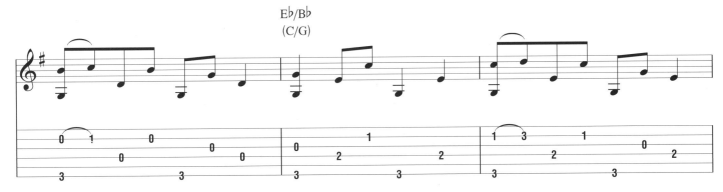

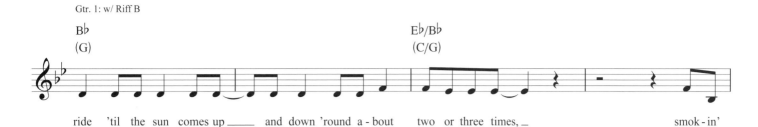

ride 'til the sun comes up ___ and down 'round a - bout two or three times, ___ smok - in'

cig - a - rettes in ___ the last seat, sing {this/my} song for the peo-ple I meet and get a -

long with it all, ___ uh, where the peo-ple say, "y'all." {I sing a/Feed the}

Gtr. 1

song with a friend, ___ change the shape that I'm in, ___ and get
pi - geons some clay, ___ turn the night in - to day, ___ and start

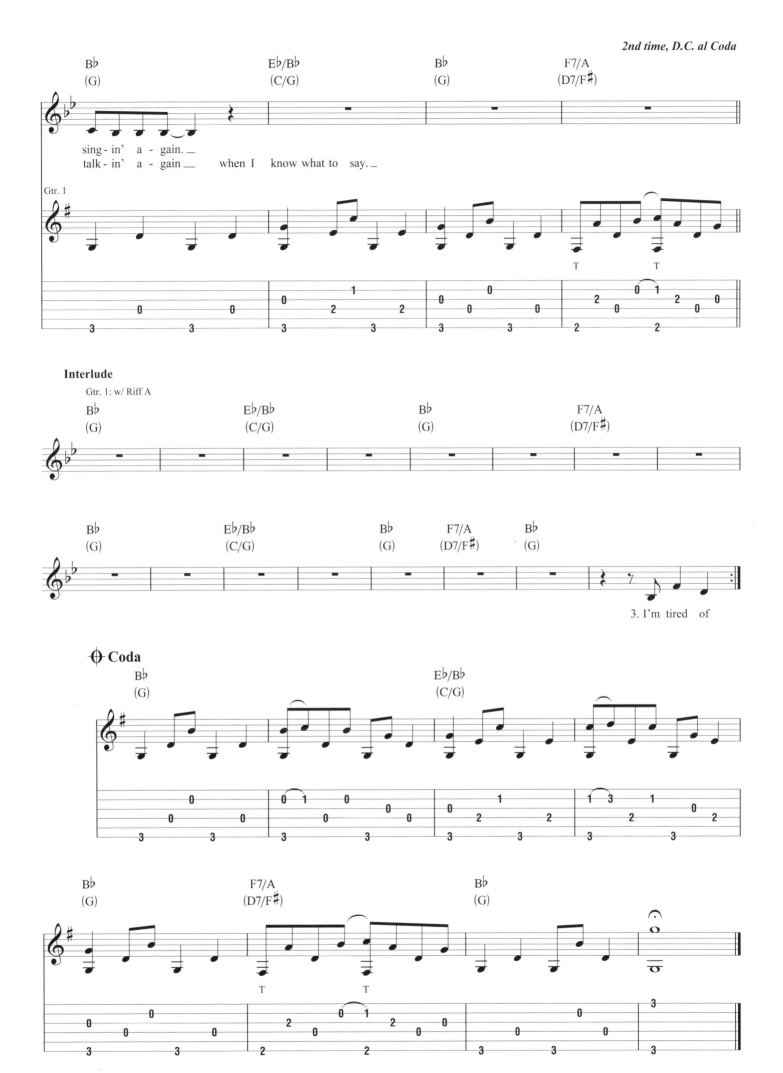

sing - in' a - gain. ___
talk - in' a - gain ___ when I know what to say. ___

Gtr. 1

**Interlude**

Gtr. 1: w/ Riff A

3. I'm tired of

**⊕ Coda**

from *Fair and Square*

# Crazy as a Loon

## Words and Music by John Prine and Pat McLaughlin

Gtr. 1: Drop D tuning:
(low to high) D-A-D-G-B-E

Gtr. 2: Capo II

**Intro**
   **Moderately** ♩ = 120

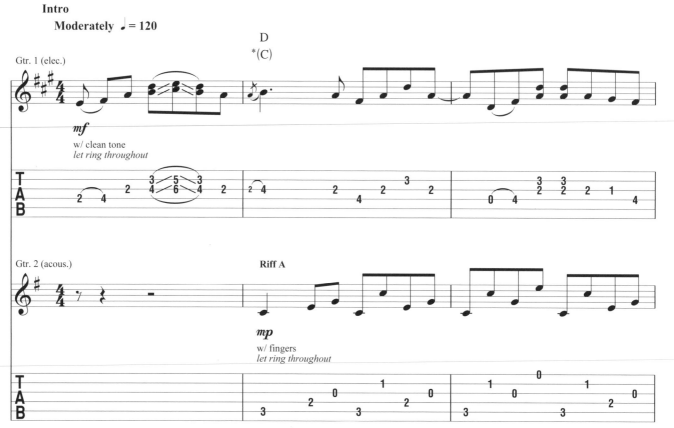

*Symbols in parentheses represent chord names respective to capoed guitar.
Symbols above reflect actual sounding chords. Capoed fret is "0" in tab.

1. Back be-fore I was a

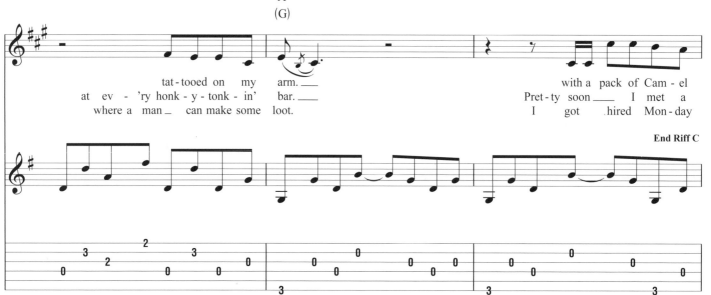

cra - zy as a loon. ___              2. So I head-ed down to

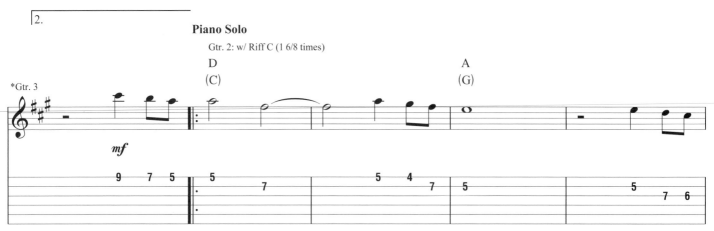

**Piano Solo**

Gtr. 2: w/ Riff C (1 6/8 times)

*Piano arr. for gtr.

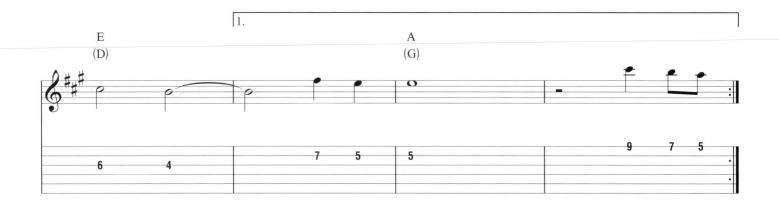

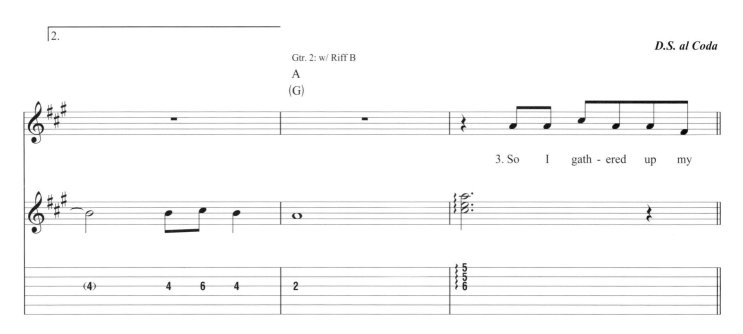

*D.S. al Coda*

Gtr. 2: w/ Riff B

3. So I gath - ered up my

**Outro**

Gtr. 2: w/ Riff C (1 6/8 times)

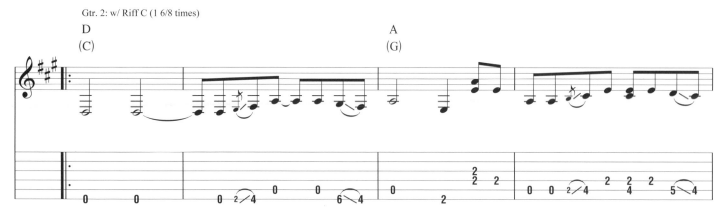

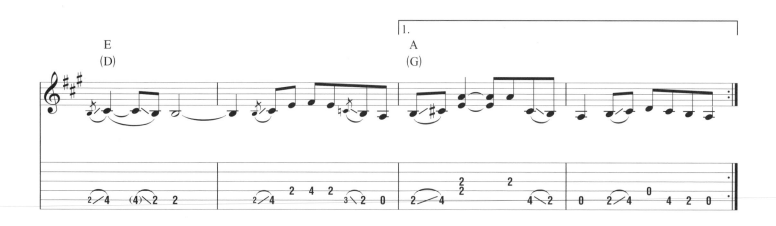

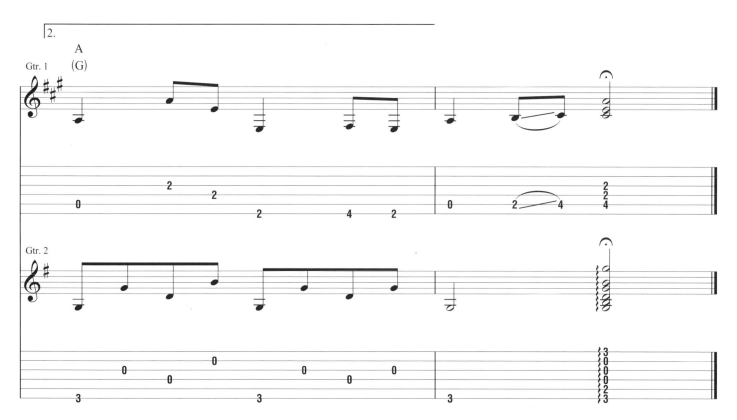

from *Sweet Revenge*

# Dear Abby

**Words and Music by John Prine**

Capo IV

**Verse**
Slow ♩. = 59

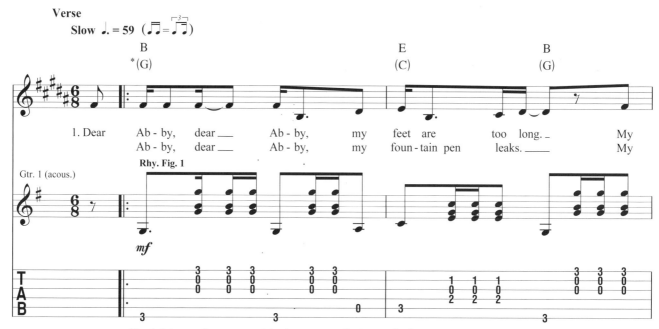

1. Dear Ab-by, dear ___ Ab-by, my feet are too long. ___ My
Ab-by, dear ___ Ab-by, my foun-tain pen leaks. ___ My

*Symbols in parentheses represent chord names respective to capoed guitar.
Symbols above reflect actual sounding chords. Capoed fret is "0" in tab.

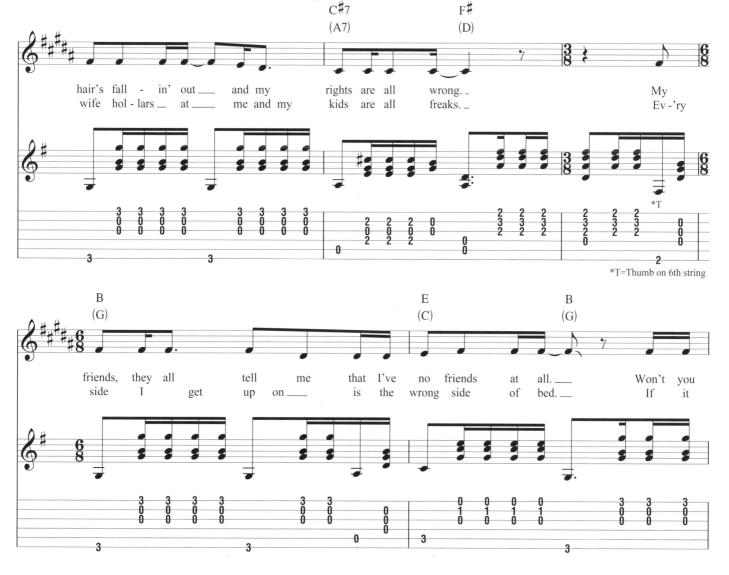

hair's fall-in' out ___ and my rights are all wrong. ___ My
wife hol-lars ___ at ___ me and my kids are all freaks. ___ Ev-'ry

*T=Thumb on 6th string

friends, they all tell me that I've no friends at all. ___ Won't you
side I get up on ___ is the wrong side of bed. ___ If it

write me a let-ter? Won't you give me a call?
weren't so ex-pen-sive, I'd wish I were dead.

**End Rhy. Fig. 1**

Signed, _____ Be-wild-ered. Be-
Signed, _____ Un-hap-py. Un-

**%Chorus**

Gtr. 1: w/ Rhy. Fig. 1 (1st 8 meas.)

wild-ered, Be-wild-ered,
hap-py, Un-hap-py, } you have ___ no com-plaint. ___ You are ___
mak-er, Noise-mak-er,

___ what you are ___ and you ain't what you ain't. ___ So

lis-ten up, ___ Bus-ter, and lis-ten up good. ___ Stop wish-in' for bad ___ luck and

knock - in' on wood.

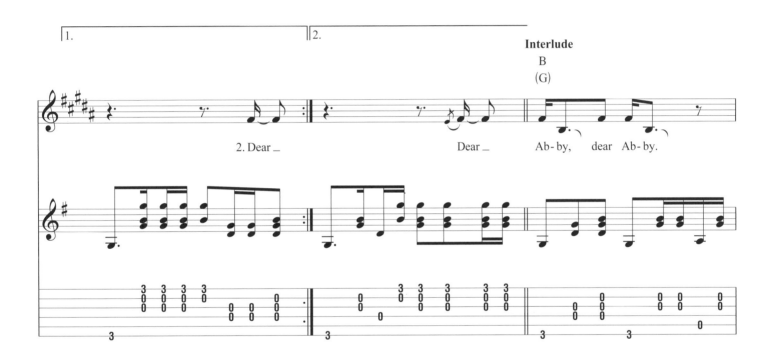

Interlude

2. Dear ___          Dear ___          Ab - by,   dear   Ab - by.

Huh,        dear Ab - by, dear   Ab - by.          Well,... ___                              3. Dear

Gtr. 1: w/ Rhy. Fig. 1

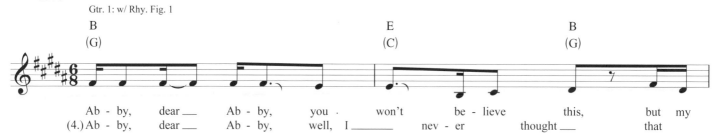

Ab - by, dear __ Ab - by, you won't be - lieve this, but my
(4.)Ab - by, dear __ Ab - by, well, I _____ nev - er thought _____ that

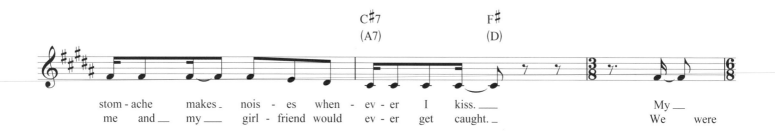

stom - ache makes nois - es when - ev - er I kiss. ___ My __
me and __ my __ girl - friend would ev - er get caught. ___ We were

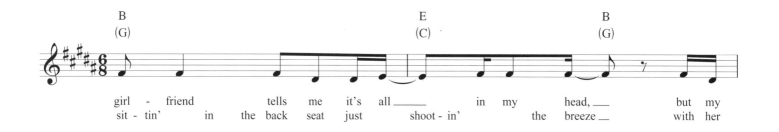

girl - friend tells me it's all _____ in my head, ___ but my
sit - tin' in the back seat just shoot - in' the breeze __ with her

stom - ache ___ tells ___ me to write ___ you in - stead.
hair up in curl - ers and ___ her pants to her knees. __

*To Coda 2* ⊕

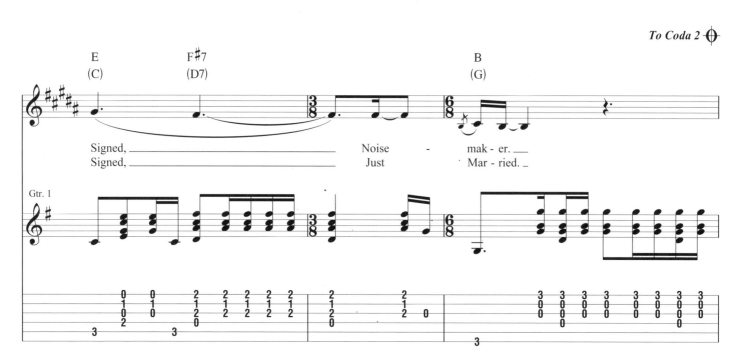

Signed, _____ Noise - mak - er. __
Signed, _____ Just Mar - ried. __

Gtr. 1

from *Bruised Orange*

# Fish and Whistle

## Words and Music by John Prine

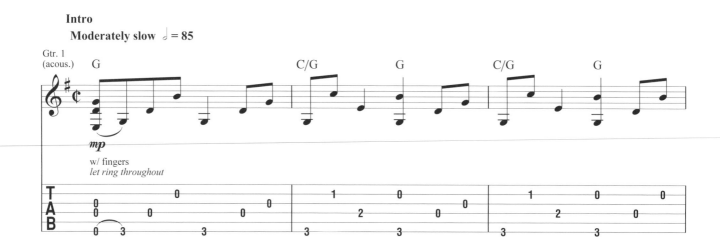

*T=Thumb on 6th string

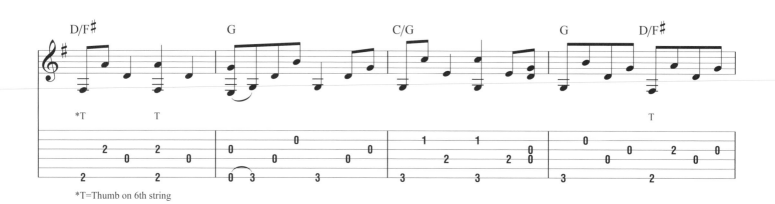

**Verse**

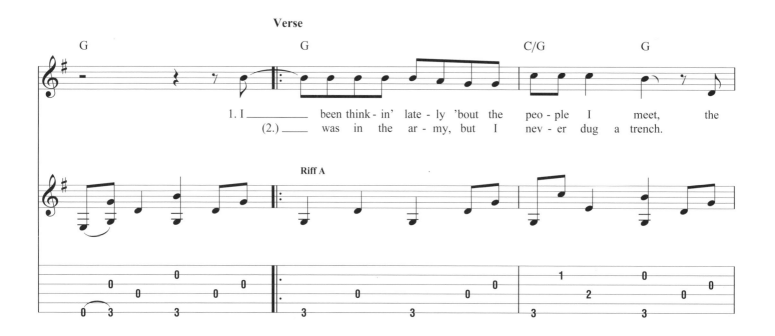

1. I _____ been think - in' late - ly 'bout the  peo - ple I  meet,  the
(2.) _____ was in the  ar - my, but I  nev - er  dug  a trench.

**Riff A**

thank you and please. They made me scrub a park-ing lot down on my knees.

Gtr. 1: w/ Riff A (last 4 meas.)

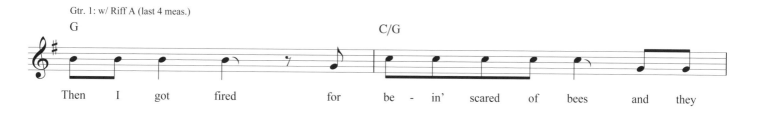

Then I got fired for be - in' scared of bees and they

D.S. al Coda 1

on - ly give me fif - ty cents an hour. _____

 **Coda 1**

**Tin Whistle Solo**

Gtr. 1: w/ Riff A

D.S.S. al Coda 2

 **Coda 2**

**Chorus**

Gtr. 1: w/ Riff A

Fath - er, for - give ___ us for what we must do. You for - give us, we'll ___

for - give you. We'll__ for - give each oth - er 'til we both turn blue, then we'll

Gtr. 1: w/ Riff A (last 2 meas., 2 times)

whis - tle and go fish - ing in heav - en. We'll whis - tle and go fish - ing in heav -

- en. We'll whis - tle and go fish - ing in heav - en.

**Interlude**

Gtr. 1

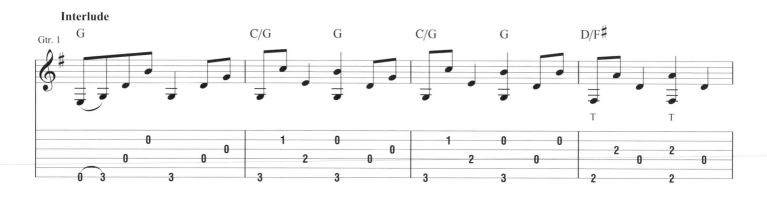

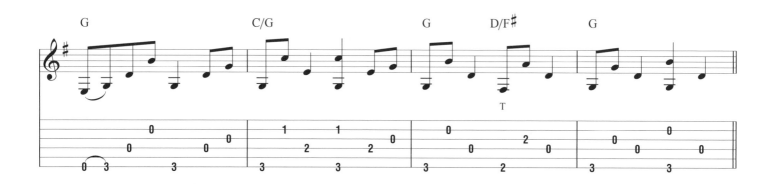

**Outro-Tin Whistle Solo**

Gtr. 1: w/ Riff A (till fade)

*Play 3 times and fade*

# Souvenirs

### Words and Music by John Prine

Capo V

**Intro**

**Moderately slow**  ♩ = 80

*Gtr. 1 (acous.)

*mf*
w/ pick & fingers
*let ring throughout*

*Three gtrs. arr. for one.

**Symbols in parentheses represent chord names respective to capoed guitar.
Symbols above reflect actual sounding chords. Capoed fret is "0" in tab.

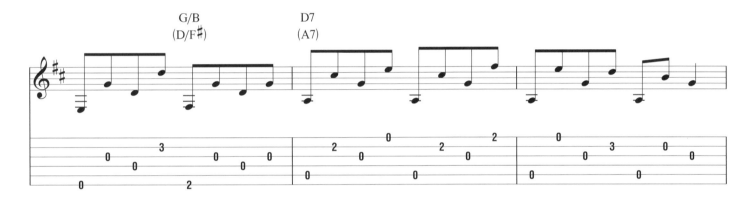

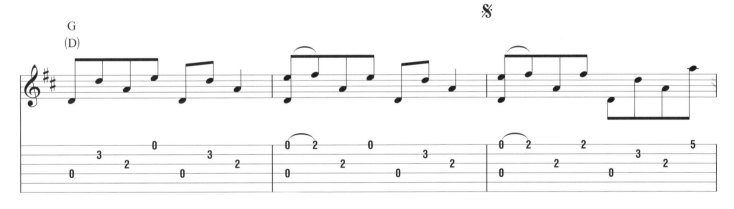

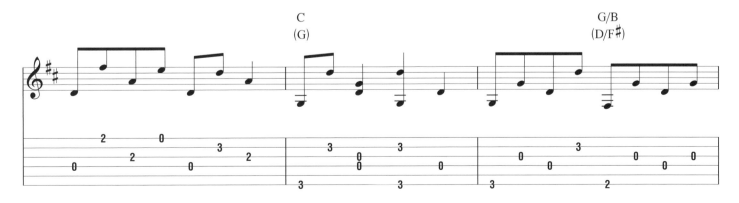

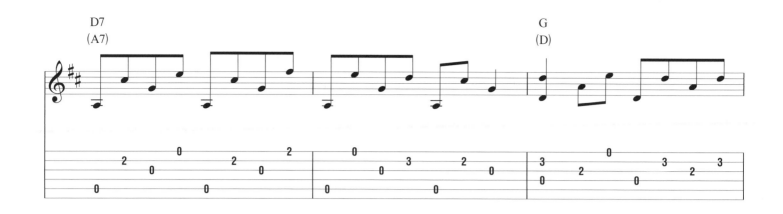

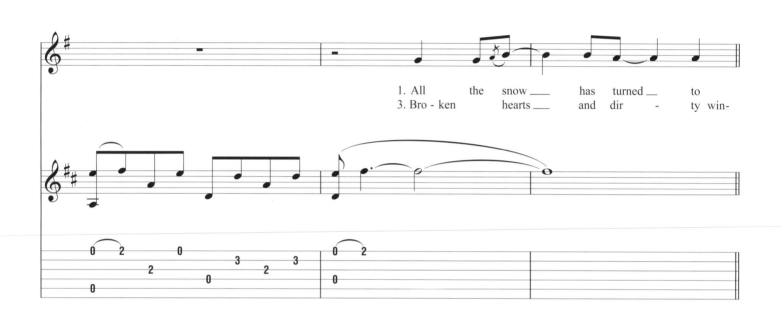

1. All the snow ___ has turned ___ to
3. Bro - ken hearts ___ and dir - ty win-

**Verse**

Csus2 (Gsus2)     G/B (D/F♯)     D7 (A7)

wat - er.
(2.) ___ shops ___
(3.) - dows
4. *See additional lyrics*

Christ - mas days ___ have come and gone. ___
for they al - ways bring me tears. ___
make life dif - fi - cult ___ to see. ___

**Riff A**                                              **End Riff A**

G
(D)

And brok - en toys ___ and fad - ed col -
I can't for - give ___ the way ___ they robbed ___
That's why last ___ night and this morn -

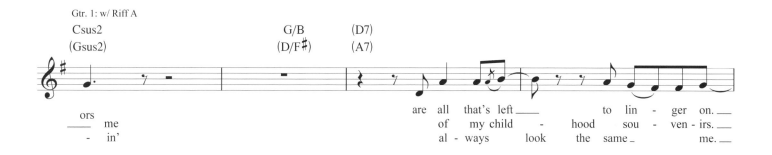

Gtr. 1: w/ Riff A

Csus2                    G/B           (D7)
(Gsus2)                  (D/F#)        (A7)

ors ___ me
___ of my child - hood sou - ven - irs. ___
- in' al - ways look the same ___ me. ___

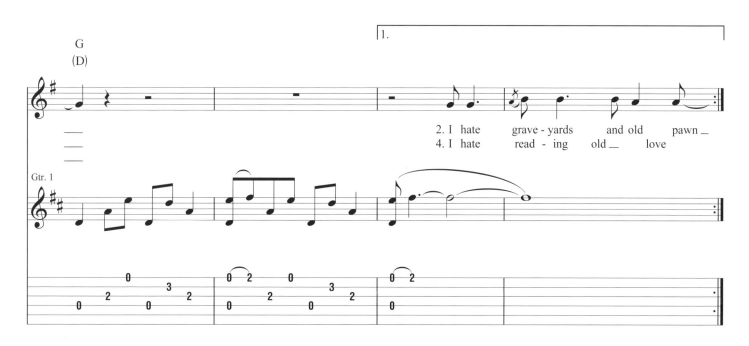

G
(D)

1.

2. I hate grave - yards and old pawn ___
4. I hate read - ing old ___ love

Gtr. 1

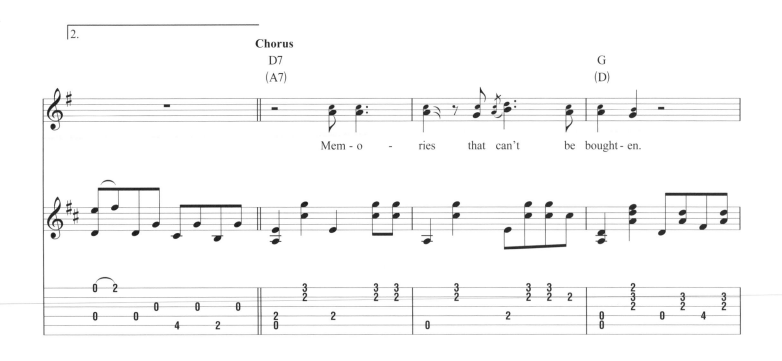

Chorus

Mem - o - ries that can't be bought - en.

They can't be won_ at car - ni - vals_ for free.

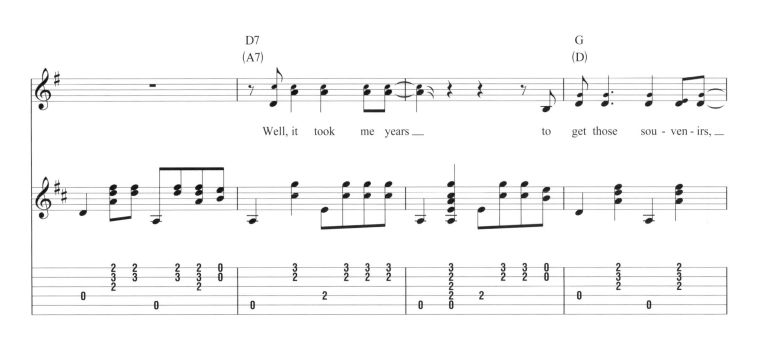

Well, it took me years _ to get those sou - ven - irs, _

*Additional Lyrics*

4. I hate reading old love letters
   For they always bring me tears.
   I can't forgive the way they rob me
   Of my sweetheart's souvenirs.

from *John Prine*

# Hello in There
## Words and Music by John Prine

Capo V

**Intro**
**Slow** ♩ = 68

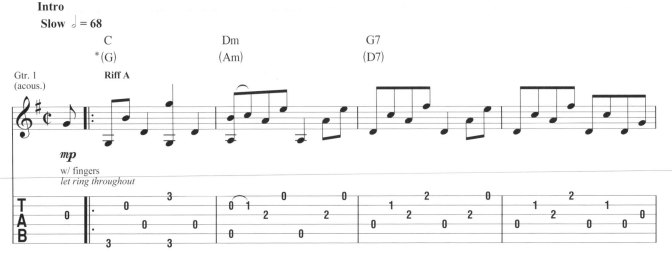

*Symbols in parentheses represent chord names respective to capoed guitar.
Symbols above reflect actual sounding chords. Capoed fret is "0" in tab.

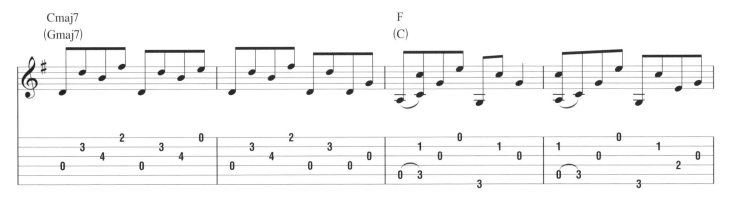

**T = Thumb on 6th string

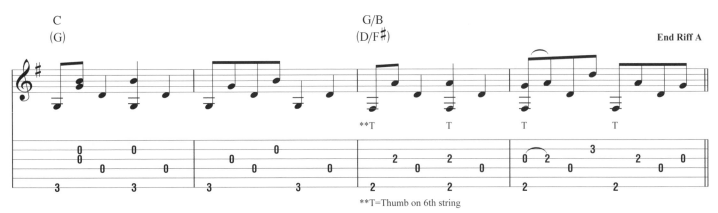

one                to say,                                        "Hel - lo   in    there, _____

*2nd time, D.S. al Coda*

_____                                        hel - lo."

**Coda**

lo   in    there, _____                                        hel - lo."

Gtr. 1

from *John Prine*
# Illegal Smile
### Words and Music by John Prine

Capo V

*Symbols in parentheses represent chord names respective to capoed guitar.
Symbols above reflect actual sounding chords. Capoed fret is "0" in tab.

**T=Thumb on 6th string

just try'n' ___ to have me some fun.

**Interlude**
**A tempo**

2. The last
3. Well, I

fun. Well done, hot dog bun, my sis-ter's a nun.

# In Spite of Ourselves

## Words and Music by John Prine

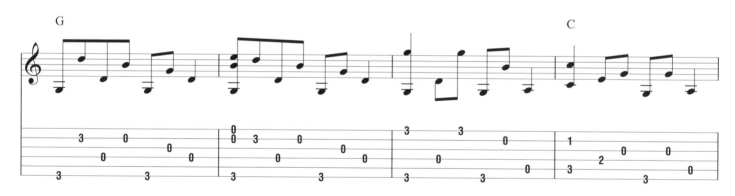

*Male:*
1. She don't like her eggs____ all run - ny.
2. She thinks all____ my jokes____ are cor - ny.

**42**

F

She thinks cros-sin' her legs ____ is fun-y.
Con - vict mov-ies make her horn-y. She looks down ___ her nose ___ She likes ketch-up on her

C

____ at mon-ey. She gets it on ___ like the Eas-ter Bun-ny.
scram-bled eggs, ___ swears like a sail-or when she shaves her legs. ___ She

G

She's my ba - by, I'm ___ her hon-ey. I'm nev-er gon-na let her go. ___
takes a lick-in' and keeps on tick-in'. I'm nev-er gon-na let her go. ___

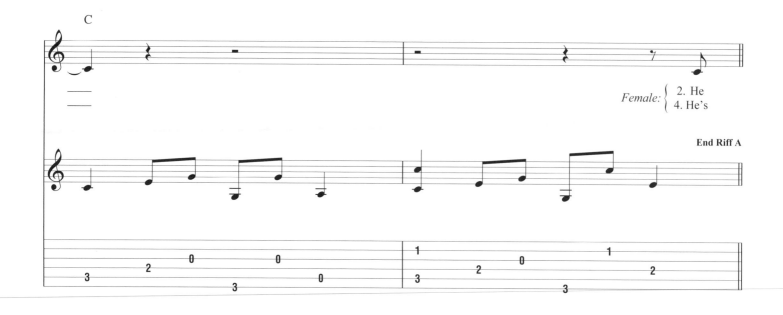

Female: 2. He / 4. He's

**End Riff A**

**Verse**

Gtr. 1: w/ Riff A

C

ain't got laid __ in a month of Sun - days. Caught him once __ and he was
got more balls __ than a big brass mon - key. (He's a) wacked - out weird - o and a

F

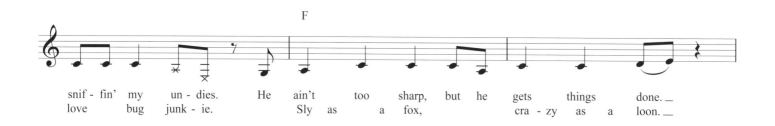

snif - fin' my un - dies. He ain't too sharp, but he gets things done. __
love bug junk - ie. Sly as a fox, cra - zy as a loon. __

C                                        G

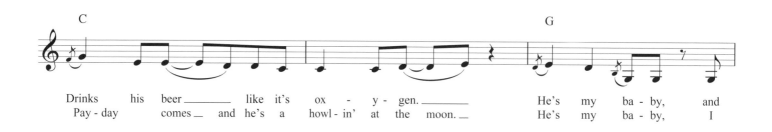

Drinks his beer _____ like it's ox - y - gen. _____ He's my ba - by, and
Pay - day comes __ and he's a howl - in' at the moon. __ He's my ba - by, I

C

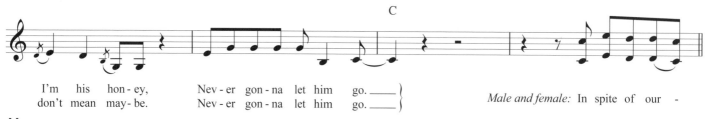

I'm his hon - ey, Nev - er gon - na let him go. __ }
don't mean may - be. Nev - er gon - na let him go. __ }

*Male and female:* In spite of our -

selves, we'll end ___ up a - sit - tin' on a rain - bow. ___ A - gainst all ___

odds, hon - ey, we're the big ___ door prize. ___ We're gon - na

spite our nos - es right off ___ of our fac - es. ___ There won't be

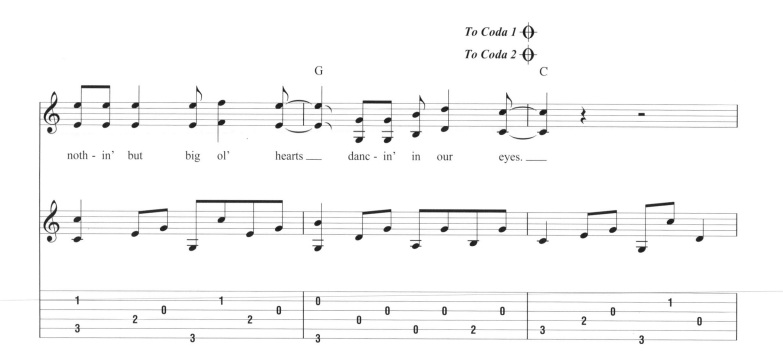

noth - in' but big ol' hearts ___ danc - in' in our eyes. ___

**Interlude**

**Coda 1**

*D.S.S. al Coda 2*

**Coda 2**

In spite of our -

There won't be noth - in' but big ol' hearts \_\_ danc - in' in our eyes. \_\_

*Spoken (male): In spite of ourselves.*

from *Fair and Square*

# Long Monday

## Words and Music by John Prine and Keith Sykes

Capo III

*Symbols in parentheses represent chord names respective to capoed guitar.
Symbols above reflect actual sounding chords. Capoed fret is "0" in tab.

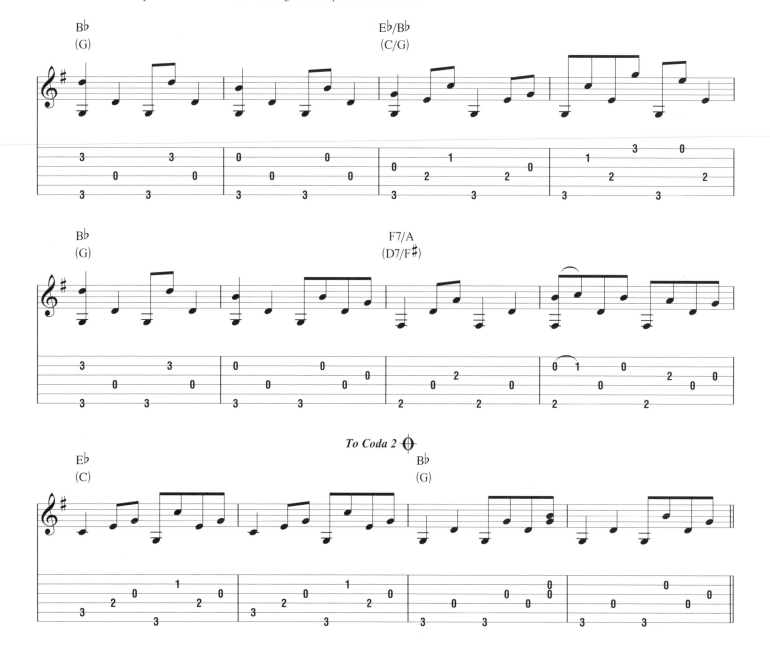

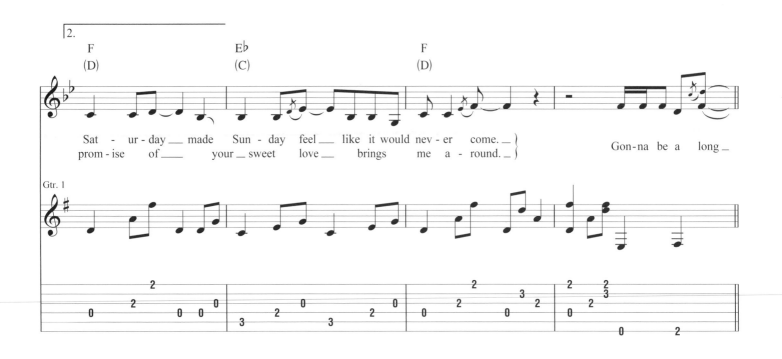

**Chorus**

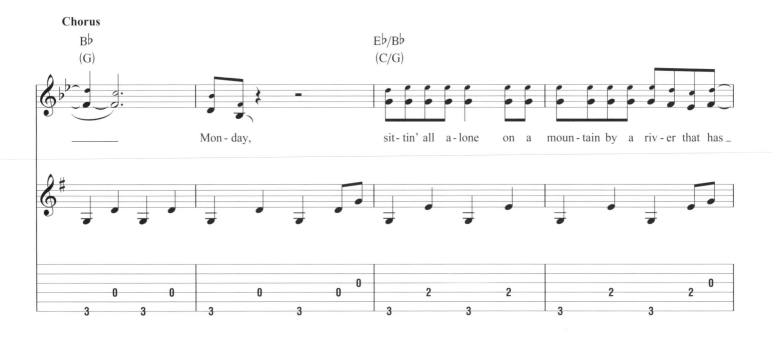

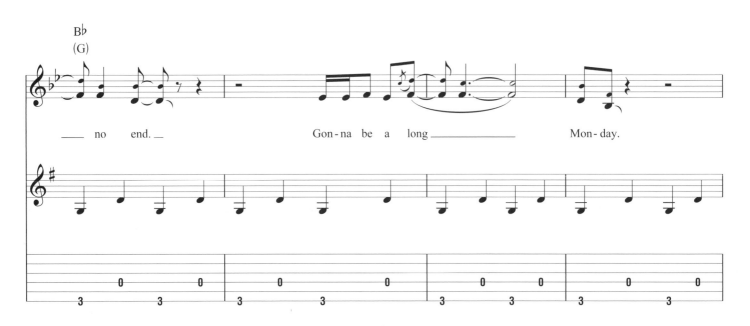

Stuck like the tick of a clock \_\_\_\_ that's come un - wound \_\_\_\_

*D.C. al Coda 1*
*(take 2nd ending)*

⊕ **Coda 1**

a - gain. \_\_\_\_

a - gain \_\_\_\_

*D.C. al Coda 2*

\_\_\_\_ and a - gain. \_\_\_\_

⊕ **Coda 2**

*rit.*

from *John Prine*

# Paradise

### Words and Music by John Prine

1. When I _____ was a child, _____ my fam - 'ly would trav - el _____ down to
(3.) coal com - p'ny came _____ with the world's larg - est shov - el _____ and they
(4.) die let my ash - es float _____ down _____ the Green Riv - er. Let my

West - ern Ken - tuck - y where my par - ents were born. _____ And there's a
tor - tured the tim - ber and stripped all the land. _____ Well, they
soul roll _____ on _____ up _____ to the Ro - ches - ter Dam. _____ I'll be

Gtr. 1: w/ Rhy. Fig. 1

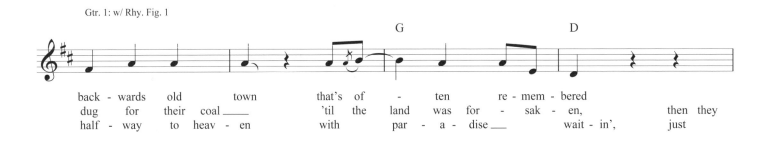

back - wards old town that's of - ten re - mem - bered
dug for their coal _____ 'til the land was for - sak - en, then they
half - way to heav - en with par - a - dise _____ wait - in', just

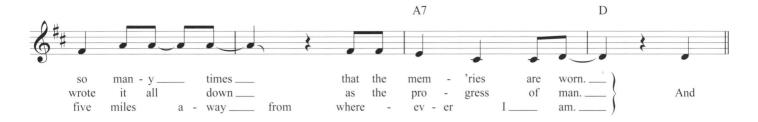

so man - y ___ times ___ that the mem - 'ries are worn. ___
wrote it all down ___ as the pro - gress of man. ___ And
five miles a - way ___ from where - ev - er I ___ am. ___

**Chorus**

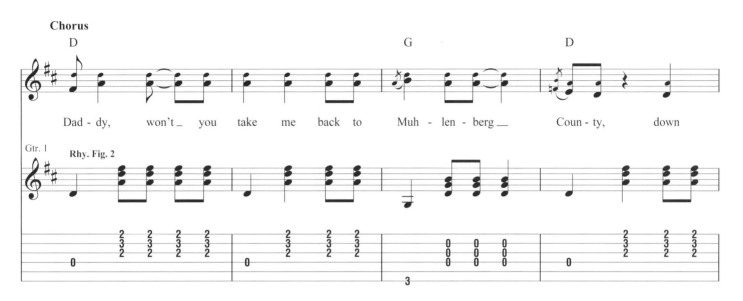

Dad - dy, won't _ you take me back to Muh - len - berg ___ Coun - ty, down

Gtr. 1 **Rhy. Fig. 2**

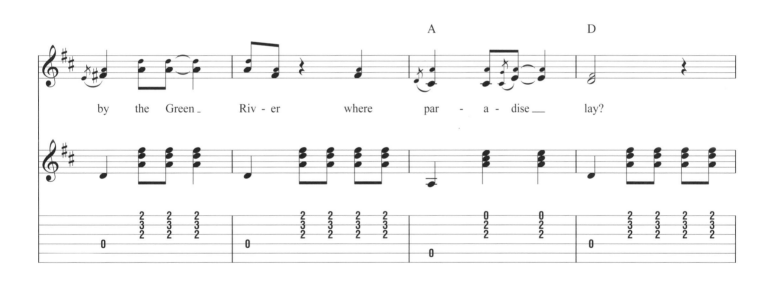

by the Green ___ Riv - er where par - a - dise ___ lay?

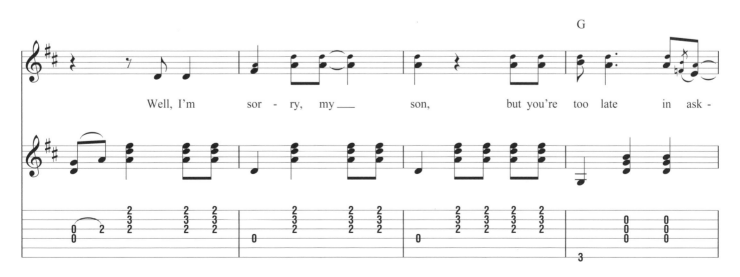

Well, I'm sor - ry, my ___ son, but you're too late in ask -

-in'.      Mis - ter   Pea - bod  -   y's   coal \_\_\_\_\_ train   has   hauled \_

*To Coda 1*

**Interlude**

\_\_\_ it   a   -   way. \_\_\_

**Verse**

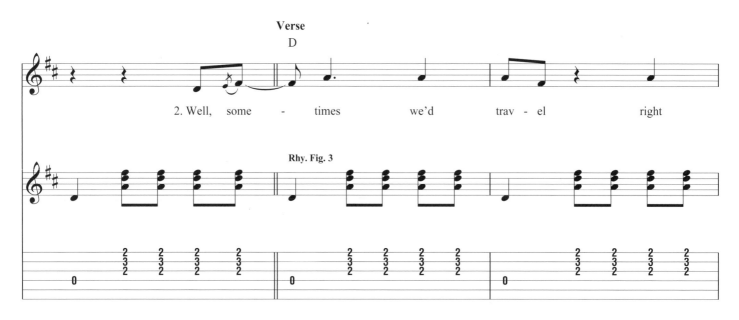

2. Well,   some   -   times   we'd   trav - el      right

down the Green\_ Riv - er to the a - ban - doned ol' \_\_\_

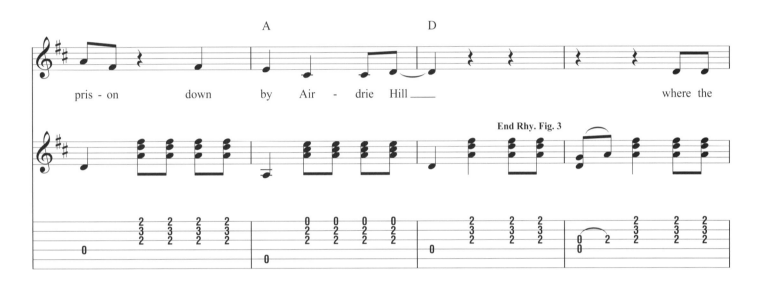

pris - on down by Air - drie Hill \_\_\_ where the

Gtr. 1: w/ Rhy. Fig. 3

air smelled like snakes and we'd shoot with our \_\_ pis - tols,   but emp-

- ty pop \_\_ bot - tles was all \_\_\_\_\_ we would\_ kill. \_\_\_\_\_ And

## Chorus

Gtr. 1: w/ Rhy. Fig. 2

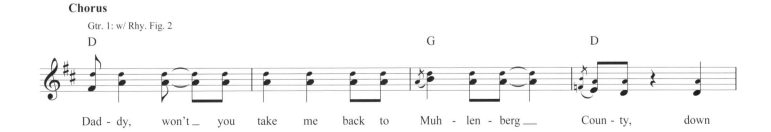

Dad - dy, won't \_ you take me back to Muh - len - berg \_\_\_ Coun - ty,   down

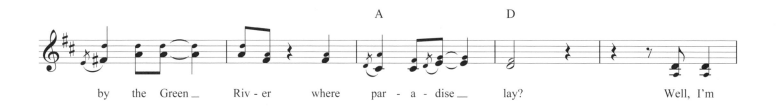

by the Green \_\_ Riv - er where par - a - dise \_\_ lay? Well, I'm

sor - ry, my \_\_\_ son, but you're too late in ask - in'.

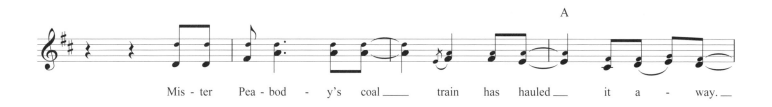

Mis - ter Pea - bod - y's coal \_\_ train has hauled \_\_ it a - way. \_\_

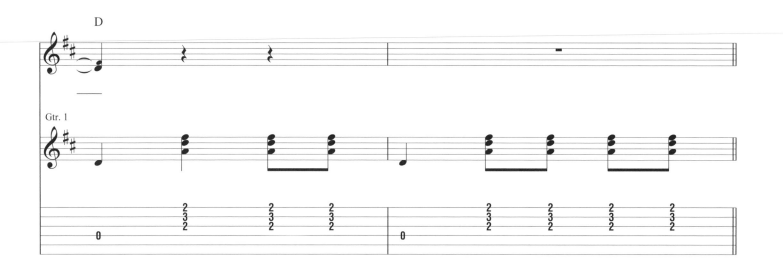

Gtr. 1

**Violin Solo**

Gtr. 1: w/ Rhy. Fig. 2 (1st 8 meas., 2 times)

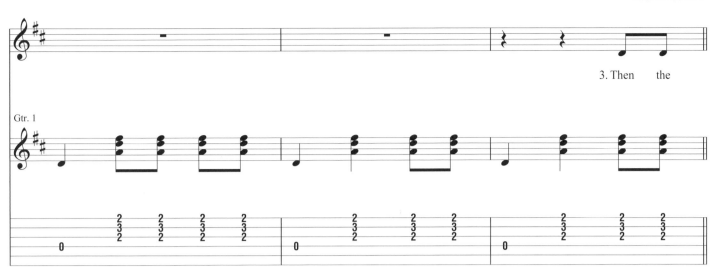

3. Then the

Gtr. 1

**Coda 1**

**Interlude**

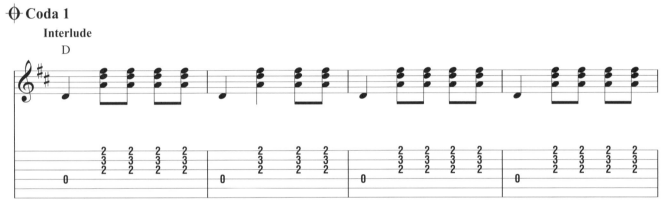

*D.S. al Coda 2*    **Coda 2**

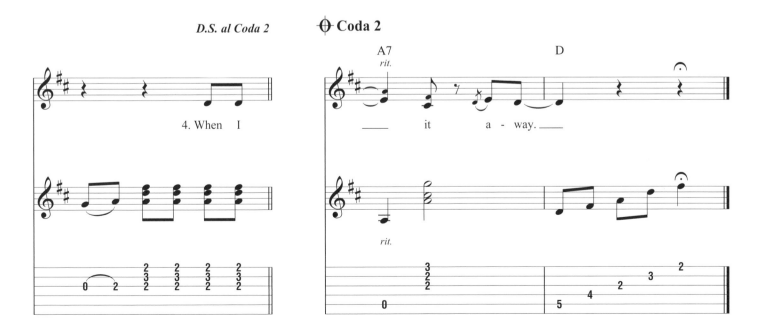

4. When I

it a - way.

# Sam Stone

**Words and Music by John Prine**

Capo V

\*\*Symbols in parentheses represent chord names respective to capoed guitar.
Symbols above reflect actual sounding chords. Capoed fret is "0" in tab.

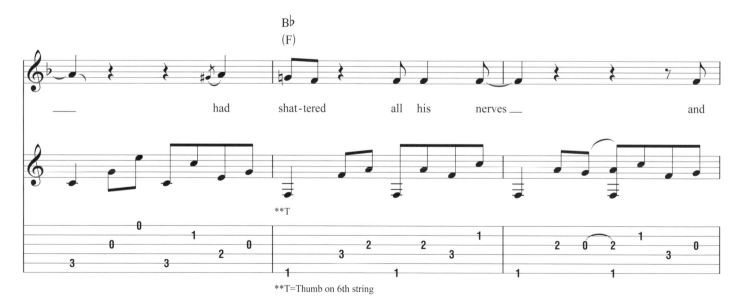

\*\*T=Thumb on 6th string

left a lit-tle shrap-nel in his knee. ___ But the mor-

**§ Pre-Chorus**

- phine eased the pain, ___ and the grass grew 'round his brain ___ and
___ rolled through his veins ___ like a thou-sand rail-road trains ___ 'n'
___ had lost its fun, ___ and there was noth-in' to be done ___ but trade ___

gave him all ___ the con-fi-dence ___ he lacked ___ with a
eased his mind ___ in the hours that he chose ___ while the
___ his house ___ that he bought on the G. I. Bill ___ for a

Pur - ple Heart __ and a mon - key on his back. ____
kids ran a - round wear - in' oth - er peo - ple's clothes. __
flag - draped cas - ket on a lo - cal he - ro's hill. ____

There's a

**Chorus**
**A tempo**

hole in dad - dy's arm __ where all __ the mon - ey goes,

and Je - sus Christ died for noth - in' I __ sup - pose. __

Lit - tle

pitch - ers have __ big ears. __ Don't stop to count the years. __

Sweet songs nev - er last __ too long __ on

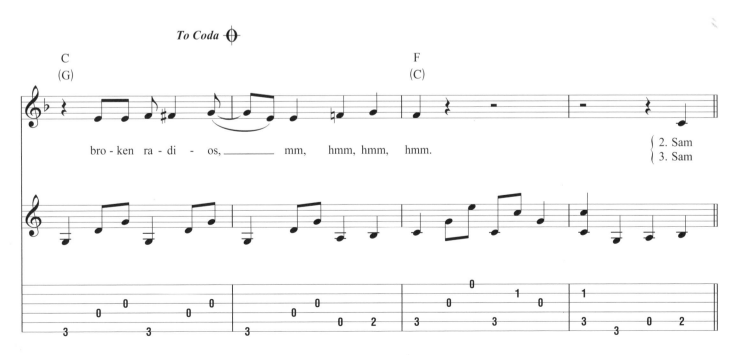

bro - ken ra - di - os, __ mm, hmm, hmm, hmm.

2. Sam
3. Sam

**Verse**

Stone's wel-come home __ did-n't __ last __ too long.
Stone was a-lone __ when he popped his __ last bal-loon, __

__ He went to work when he'd spent his __ last dime. __
climb-in' walls while sit-ting in a chair. __

__ And Sam-my took to steal-in' when he got __
__ Well, he played his last __ re-quest __ while the

*2nd time, D.S. al Coda*

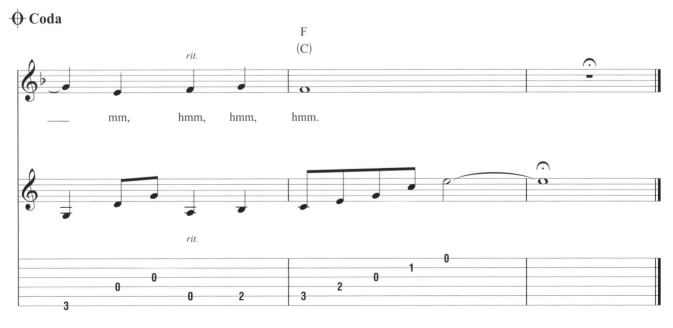

from *John Prine*

# Spanish Pipedream

**Words and Music by John Prine and Jeff Kent**

*Symbols in parentheses represent chord names respective to capoed guitar.
Symbols above reflect actual sounding chords. Capoed fret is "0" in tab.

pressed her chest __ a - gainst __ me    a - bout the time the juke __ box
danced a - round __ the bar __ room    and she did the hooch - y   coo. __
"You must    know    the an - swer."   She said, "No,   but I'll give it a    try." __

broke.    Yeah, she gim - me a peck __ on    the back of her neck, __    and
__    Yeah, she sang her    song __    all __ night    long, __
__    And to this ver - y day, __    we been    liv - in' our way; __

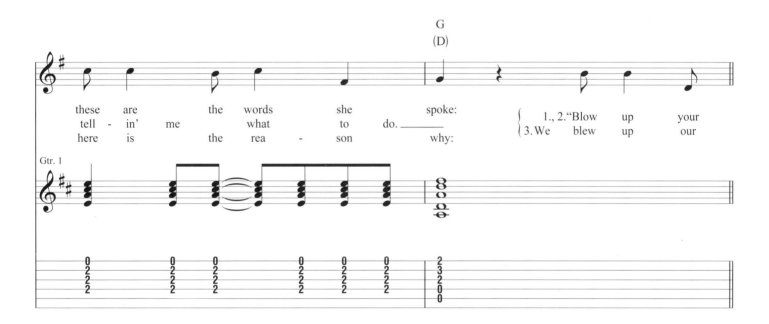

these are    the words    she    spoke:    { 1., 2."Blow    up    your
tell - in' me    what    to    do. __    { 3. We blew    up    our
here is    the rea - son    why:

Gtr. 1

Chorus

T - V,    throw __ a - way your pa - per,    go __ to the
T - V,    threw __ a - way our pa - per,    went __ to the

Rhy. Fig. 2

from *Sweet Revenge*

# Sweet Revenge

### Words and Music by John Prine

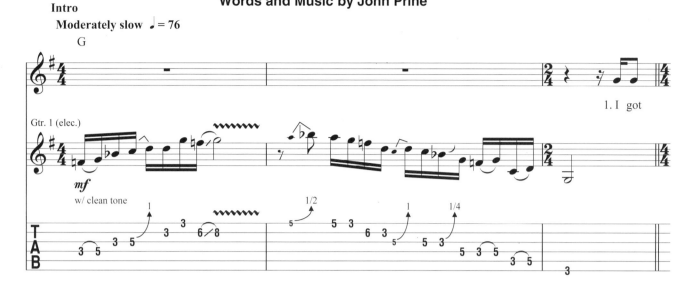

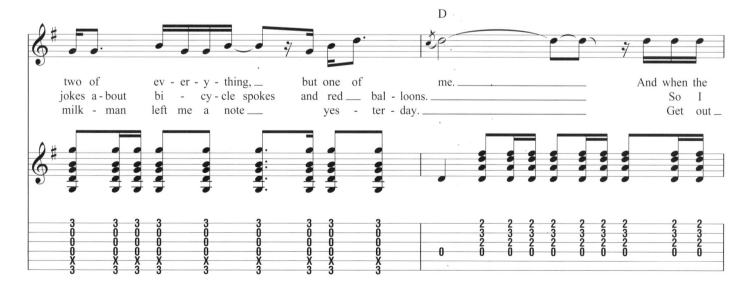

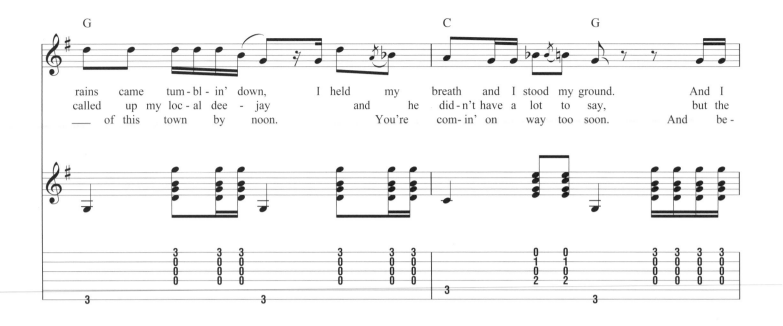

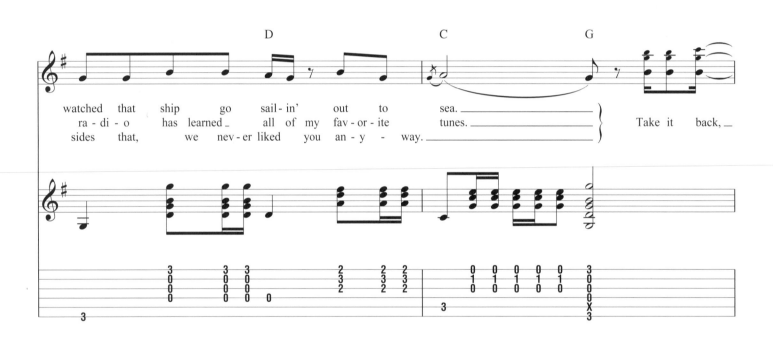

**Chorus**

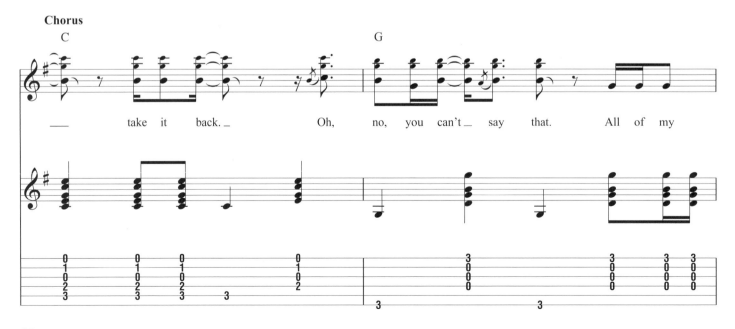

from *Bruised Orange*

# That's the Way the World Goes 'Round

## Words and Music by John Prine

Capo V

**Intro**
**Moderately slow** ♩ = 78

*Symbols in parentheses represent chord names respective
to capoed guitar. Symbols above reflect actual sounding chords.
Capoed fret is "0" in tab.

**T=Thumb on 6th string

**Verse**

1. I know a guy __ that's got a lot to lose. __ He's a pret - ty nice fel - la,

kind - a con - fused. __ Got mus - cles in his head, ain't nev - er been used, __ thinks __

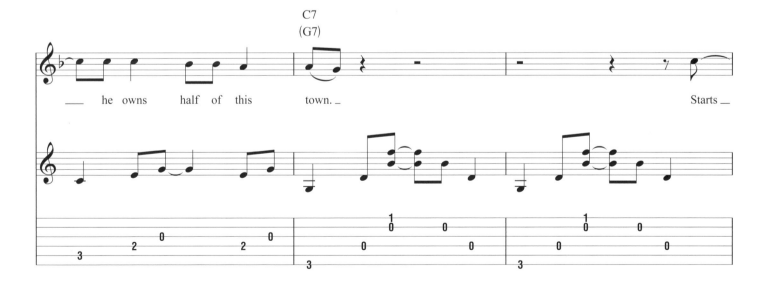

__ he owns half of this town. __ Starts __

Gtr. 1: w/ Riff B

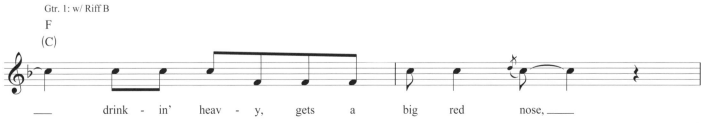

__ drink - in' heav - y, gets a big red nose, __

beats his old la - dy with a rub - ber hose, ___ then he

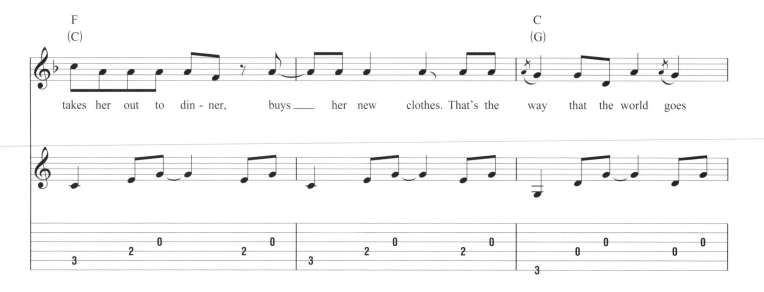

takes her out to din - ner, buys ___ her new clothes. That's the way that the world goes

♪ Chorus

'round. That's the way ___ that the world goes 'round. ___ You're

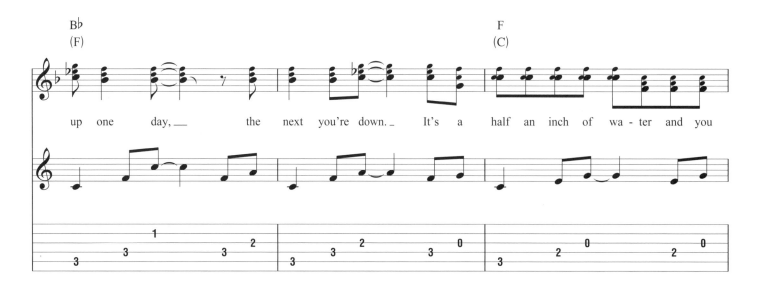

up one day, ___ the next you're down. ___ It's a half an inch of wa - ter and you

# GUITAR NOTATION LEGEND

Guitar music can be notated three different ways: on a *musical staff*, in *tablature*, and in *rhythm slashes*.

**RHYTHM SLASHES** are written above the staff. Strum chords in the rhythm indicated. Use the chord diagrams found at the top of the first page of the transcription for the appropriate chord voicings. Round noteheads indicate single notes.

**THE MUSICAL STAFF** shows pitches and rhythms and is divided by bar lines into measures. Pitches are named after the first seven letters of the alphabet.

**TABLATURE** graphically represents the guitar fingerboard. Each horizontal line represents a string, and each number represents a fret.

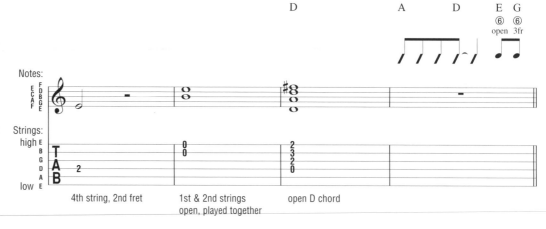

4th string, 2nd fret     1st & 2nd strings open, played together     open D chord

# Definitions for Special Guitar Notation

**HALF-STEP BEND:** Strike the note and bend up 1/2 step.

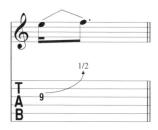

**WHOLE-STEP BEND:** Strike the note and bend up one step.

**GRACE NOTE BEND:** Strike the note and immediately bend up as indicated.

**SLIGHT (MICROTONE) BEND:** Strike the note and bend up 1/4 step.

**BEND AND RELEASE:** Strike the note and bend up as indicated, then release back to the original note. Only the first note is struck.

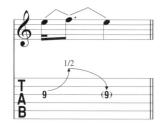

**PRE-BEND:** Bend the note as indicated, then strike it.

**PRE-BEND AND RELEASE:** Bend the note as indicated. Strike it and release the bend back to the original note.

**UNISON BEND:** Strike the two notes simultaneously and bend the lower note up to the pitch of the higher.

**VIBRATO:** The string is vibrated by rapidly bending and releasing the note with the fretting hand.

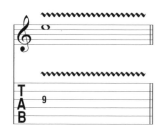

**WIDE VIBRATO:** The pitch is varied to a greater degree by vibrating with the fretting hand.

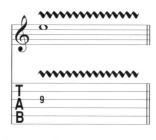

**HAMMER-ON:** Strike the first (lower) note with one finger, then sound the higher note (on the same string) with another finger by fretting it without picking.

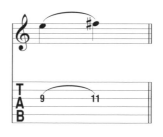

**PULL-OFF:** Place both fingers on the notes to be sounded. Strike the first note and without picking, pull the finger off to sound the second (lower) note.

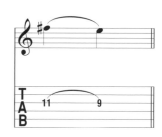

**LEGATO SLIDE:** Strike the first note and then slide the same fret-hand finger up or down to the second note. The second note is not struck.

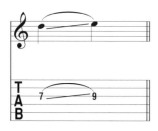

**SHIFT SLIDE:** Same as legato slide, except the second note is struck.

**TRILL:** Very rapidly alternate between the notes indicated by continuously hammering on and pulling off.

**TAPPING:** Hammer ("tap") the fret indicated with the pick-hand index or middle finger and pull off to the note fretted by the fret hand.

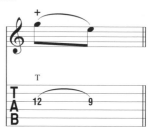

**NATURAL HARMONIC:** Strike the note while the fret-hand lightly touches the string directly over the fret indicated.

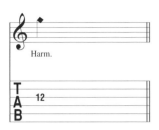

Harm.

**PINCH HARMONIC:** The note is fretted normally and a harmonic is produced by adding the edge of the thumb or the tip of the index finger of the pick hand to the normal pick attack.

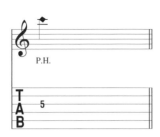

P.H.

**HARP HARMONIC:** The note is fretted normally and a harmonic is produced by gently resting the pick hand's index finger directly above the indicated fret (in parentheses) while the pick hand's thumb or pick assists by plucking the appropriate string.

H.H.

**PICK SCRAPE:** The edge of the pick is rubbed down (or up) the string, producing a scratchy sound.

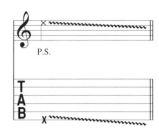

P.S.

**MUFFLED STRINGS:** A percussive sound is produced by laying the fret hand across the string(s) without depressing, and striking them with the pick hand.

**PALM MUTING:** The note is partially muted by the pick hand lightly touching the string(s) just before the bridge.

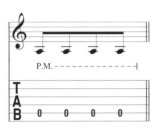

P.M.

**RAKE:** Drag the pick across the strings indicated with a single motion.

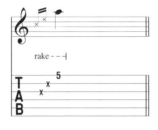

rake

**TREMOLO PICKING:** The note is picked as rapidly and continuously as possible.

**ARPEGGIATE:** Play the notes of the chord indicated by quickly rolling them from bottom to top.

**VIBRATO BAR DIVE AND RETURN:** The pitch of the note or chord is dropped a specified number of steps (in rhythm), then returned to the original pitch.

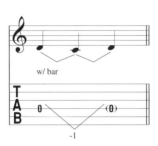

w/ bar

**VIBRATO BAR SCOOP:** Depress the bar just before striking the note, then quickly release the bar.

w/ bar

**VIBRATO BAR DIP:** Strike the note and then immediately drop a specified number of steps, then release back to the original pitch.

w/ bar

# Additional Musical Definitions

| | | |
|---|---|---|
|  (accent) | • Accentuate note (play it louder). | |
| (accent) | • Accentuate note with great intensity. | |
| (staccato) | • Play the note short. | |
| ⊓ | • Downstroke | |
| V | • Upstroke | |
| *D.S. al Coda* | • Go back to the sign (𝄋), then play until the measure marked "*To Coda*," then skip to the section labelled "**Coda**." | |
| *D.C. al Fine* | • Go back to the beginning of the song and play until the measure marked "*Fine*" (end). | |

**Rhy. Fig.** — • Label used to recall a recurring accompaniment pattern (usually chordal).

**Riff** — • Label used to recall composed, melodic lines (usually single notes) which recur.

**Fill** — • Label used to identify a brief melodic figure which is to be inserted into the arrangement.

**Rhy. Fill** — • A chordal version of a Fill.

tacet — • Instrument is silent (drops out).

 — • Repeat measures between signs.

 — • When a repeated section has different endings, play the first ending only the first time and the second ending only the second time.

**NOTE:** Tablature numbers in parentheses mean:
1. The note is being sustained over a system (note in standard notation is tied), or
2. The note is sustained, but a new articulation (such as a hammer-on, pull-off, slide or vibrato) begins, or
3. The note is a barely audible "ghost" note (note in standard notation is also in parentheses).

# GUITAR RECORDED VERSIONS®

Guitar Recorded Versions® are note-for-note transcriptions of guitar music taken directly off recordings. This series, one of the most popular in print today, features some of the greatest guitar players and groups from blues and rock to country and jazz.

Guitar Recorded Versions are transcribed by the best transcribers in the business. Every book contains notes and tablature unless otherwise marked. Visit **halleonard.com** for our complete selection.

**AUTHENTIC TRANSCRIPTIONS
WITH NOTES AND TABLATURE**

**Will Ackerman**
00690016  The Will Ackerman
Collection ..........................$22.99

**Bryan Adams**
00690501  Greatest Hits ............$24.99

**Aerosmith**
00690002  Big Ones .................$24.95
00690603  O Yeah! ...................$27.99

**Alice in Chains**
00690178  Acoustic .................$19.99
00694865  Dirt .......................$19.99
00660225  Facelift ...................$19.99
00694925  Jar of Flies/Sap .....$19.99
00690387  Nothing Safe ...........$24.99

**All That Remains**
00142819  The Order of Things..$22.99

**Allman Brothers Band**
00694932  Definitive Collection,
Volume 1..................$27.99
00694933  Definitive Collection,
Volume 2..................$27.99
00694934  Definitive Collection,
Volume 3..................$29.99

**Duane Allman**
00690958  Guitar Anthology ......$29.99

**Alter Bridge**
00691071  AB III ....................$29.99
00690945  Blackbird ................$24.99
00690755  One Day Remains......$24.99

**Anthrax**
00690849  Best of Anthrax..........$19.99

**Arctic Monkeys**
00123558  AM ........................$24.99

**Chet Atkins**
00690158  Almost Alone ............$22.99
00694876  Contemporary Styles...$19.95
00694878  Vintage Fingerstyle.....$19.99

**Audioslave**
00690609  Audioslave................$24.99
00690884  Revelations .............$19.95

**Avenged Sevenfold**
00690926  Avenged Sevenfold ....$24.99
00214869  Best of: 2005-2013 ..$24.99
00690820  City of Evil .............$24.95
00123216  Hail to the King .......$22.99
00691051  Nightmare ...............$22.99
00222486  The Stage ...............$24.99
00691065  Waking the Fallen.....$22.99

**The Avett Brothers**
00123140  Guitar Collection ......$22.99

**Randy Bachman**
00694918  Guitar Collection.......$22.95

**The Beatles**
00690489  1 (Number Ones) .....$24.99
00694929  1962-1966 .............$24.99
00694930  1967-1970 .............$27.99
00694880  Abbey Road............$19.99
00694832  Acoustic Guitar.........$24.99
00691066  Beatles for Sale .......$22.99
00690903  Capitol Albums Vol. 2 .$24.99
00691031  Help! .....................$19.99
00690482  Let It Be .................$19.99
00691030  Magical Mystery Tour..$22.99
00691067  Meet the Beatles! ......$22.99
00691068  Please Please Me ......$22.99
00694891  Revolver .................$19.99
00691014  Rock Band ..............$34.99
00694863  Rubber Soul ............$22.99
00694863  Sgt. Pepper's Lonely
Hearts Club Band ......$22.99
00110193  Tomorrow
Never Knows ..........$22.99
00690110  White Album Book 1..$19.99
00690111  White Album Book 2..$19.99
00690383  Yellow Submarine .....$19.95

**The Beach Boys**
00690503  Very Best ...................$24.99

**Beck**
00690632  Beck – Sea Change ...$19.95

**Jeff Beck**
00691044  Best of Beck.............$24.99
00691042  Blow by Blow............$22.99
00691041  Truth ......................$19.99
00691043  Wired......................$19.99

**George Benson**
00694884  Best of ...................$22.99

**Chuck Berry**
00692385  Chuck Berry .............$22.99

**Billy Talent**
00690835  Billy Talent ..............$22.99
00690879  Billy Talent II............$19.99

**Black Crowes**
00147787  Best of ....................$19.99

**The Black Keys**
00129737  Turn Blue ................$22.99

**Black Sabbath**
00690149  Black Sabbath ..........$17.99
00690901  Best of ...................$22.99
00691010  Heaven and Hell ......$22.99
00690148  Master of Reality ......$19.99
00690142  Paranoid .................$17.99
00690145  Vol. 4 ....................$22.99
00692200  We Sold Our Soul
for Rock 'n' Roll ......$22.99

**blink-182**
00690389  Enema of the State ....$19.95
00690831  Greatest Hits............$24.99
00691179  Neighborhoods..........$22.99

**Michael Bloomfield**
00148544  Guitar Anthology ......$24.99

**Blue Öyster Cult**
00690028  Cult Classics .............$19.99

**Bon Jovi**
00691074  Greatest Hits...........$24.99

**Joe Bonamassa**
00158600  Blues of Desperation $22.99
00139086  Different Shades
of Blue ..................$22.99
00198117  Muddy Wolf at
Red Rocks .............$24.99
00283540  Redemption .............$24.99

**Boston**
00690913  Boston....................$19.99
00690932  Don't Look Back .......$19.99
00690829  Guitar Collection ......$24.99

**David Bowie**
00690491  Best of ...................$19.99

**Box Car Racer**
00690583  Box Car Racer..........$19.95

**Breaking Benjamin**
00691023  Dear Agony .............$22.99
00690873  Phobia....................$19.99

**Lenny Breau**
00141446  Best of ...................$19.99

**Big Bill Broonzy**
00286503  Guitar Collection ......$19.99

**Roy Buchanan**
00690168  Collection ...............$24.99

**Jeff Buckley**
00690451  Collection................$24.99

**Bullet for My Valentine**
00691047  Fever .....................$22.99
00690957  Scream Aim Fire .......$22.99
00119629  Temper Temper ........$22.99

**Kenny Burrell**
00690678  Best of ...................$22.99

**Cage the Elephant**
00691077  Thank You,
Happy Birthday ........$22.99

**The Cars**
00691159  Complete Greatest Hits.$22.99

**Carter Family**
00690261  Collection................$19.99

**Johnny Cash**
00691079  Best of ...................$22.99

**Cheap Trick**
00690043  Best of....................$19.95

**Chicago**
00690171  Definitive
Guitar Collection ......$24.99

**Chimaira**
00691011  Guitar Collection ......$24.99

**Charlie Christian**
00690567  Definitive Collection ..$22.99

**Eric Church**
00101916  Chief .....................$22.99

**The Civil Wars**
00129545  The Civil Wars .........$19.99

**Eric Clapton**
00690590  Anthology .................$34.99
00692391  Best of....................$22.95
00694896  Blues Breakers
(with John Mayall) ....$19.99
00138731  The Breeze .............$22.99
00691055  Clapton ..................$22.99
00690936  Complete Clapton .....$29.99
00690010  From the Cradle.......$22.99
00192383  I Still Do ................$19.99
00690363  Just One Night .........$24.99
00694873  Timepieces .............$19.95
00694869  Unplugged ...............$24.99
00124873  Unplugged (Deluxe) ..$29.99

**The Clash**
00690162  Best of ...................$19.99

**Coheed & Cambria**
00690828  IV .........................$19.95
00139967  In Keeping Secrets of
Silent Earth: 3 ..........$24.99

**Coldplay**
00130786  Ghost Stories ..........$19.99
00690593  A Rush of Blood
to the Head .............$19.95

**Collective Soul**
00690855  Best of ...................$19.95

**Jessee Cook**
00141704  Works Vol. 1 ...........$19.99

**Alice Cooper**
00691091  Best of....................$24.99

**Counting Crows**
00694940  August &
Everything After.........$19.99

**Robert Cray**
00127184  Best of....................$19.99

**Cream**
00694840  Disraeli Gears ..........$24.99

**Creed**
00288787  Greatest Hits.............$22.99

**Creedence Clearwater Revival**
00690819  Best of....................$24.99

**Jim Croce**
00690648  The Very Best ..........$19.99

**Steve Cropper**
00690572  Soul Man ................$22.99

**Crosby, Stills & Nash**
00690613  Best of...................$29.99

**Cry of Love**
00691171  Brother ..................$22.99

**Dick Dale**
00690637  Best of....................$19.99

**Daughtry**
00690892  Daughtry .................$19.95

**Alex de Grassi**
00690822  Best of....................$19.95

**Death Cab for Cutie**
00690967  Narrow Stairs ...........$22.99

**Deep Purple**
00690289  Best of....................$22.99
00690288  Machine Head ..........$19.99

**Def Leppard**
00690784  Best of....................$24.99

**Derek and the Dominos**
00694831  Layla & Other
Assorted Love Songs..$24.99

**Ani DiFranco**
00690384  Best of....................$19.95

**Dinosaur Jr.**
00690979  Best of....................$22.99

**The Doors**
00690347  Anthology .................$22.95
00690348  Essential Collection ...$16.95

**Dream Theater**
00160579  The Astonishing ........$24.99
00122443  Dream Theater ..........$24.99
00291164  Distance Over Time ..$24.99

**Eagles**
00278631  Their Greatest
Hits 1971-1975........$22.99
00278632  Very Best of..............$34.99

**Duane Eddy**
00690250  Best of ....................$19.99

**Tommy Emmanuel**
00147067  All I Want for
Christmas................$19.99
00690909  Best of ...................$24.99
00172824  It's Never Too Late ....$22.99
00139220  Little by Little ..........$24.99

**Melissa Etheridge**
00690555  Best of ...................$19.95

**Evanescence**
00691186  Evanescence.............$22.99

**Extreme**
00690515  Pornograffitti............$24.99

**John Fahey**
00150257  Guitar Anthology ......$19.99

**Tal Farlow**
00125661  Best of....................$19.99

**Five Finger Death Punch**
00691009  5 Finger Death Punch $19.99
00691181  American Capitalism..$22.99
00128917  Wrong Side of Heaven &
Righteous Side of Hell.$22.99

**Fleetwood Mac**
00690664  Best of....................$24.99

**Flyleaf**
00690870  Flyleaf....................$19.95

**Foghat**
00690986  Best of....................$22.99

**Foo Fighters**
00691024  Greatest Hits............$22.99
00691115  Wasting Light............$22.99

**Peter Frampton**
00690842  Best of....................$22.99

**Robben Ford**
00690805  Best of....................$24.99
00120220  Guitar Anthology .......$29.99

**Free**
00694920  Best of ...................$19.99

**Rory Gallagher**
00295410  Blues (Selections).....$24.99

**Danny Gatton**
00694807  88 Elmira St ...........$22.99

**Genesis**
00690438  Guitar Anthology .......$24.99

**Godsmack**
00120167  Godsmack.................$19.95
00691048  The Oracle ..............$22.99

**Goo Goo Dolls**
00690943  Greatest Hits Vol. 1....$24.99

**Grateful Dead**
00139460  Guitar Anthology .......$29.99

**Green Day**
00212480  Revolution Radio ......$19.99
00118259  ¡Tré! .....................$21.99
00113073  ¡Uno! .....................$21.99

**Peter Green**
00691190  Best of ...................$24.99

**Greta Van Fleet**
00287517  Anthem of the
Peaceful Army .........$19.99
00287515  From the Fires..........$19.99

**Patty Griffin**
00690927  Children Running
Through ..................$19.95

**Guns N' Roses**
00690978  Chinese Democracy...$24.99

**Buddy Guy**
00691027  Anthology ................$24.99
00694854  Damn Right, I've
Got the Blues............$19.95

**Jim Hall**
00690697  Best of....................$19.99

**Ben Harper**
00690840  Both Sides of the Gun .$19.95
00691018  Fight for Your Mind...$22.99

**George Harrison**
00694798  Anthology................$22.99

**Scott Henderson**
00690841  Blues Guitar Collection$24.99

**Jimi Hendrix**
00692930  Are You Experienced?..$27.99
00692931  Axis: Bold As Love ....$24.99
00690304  Band of Gypsys.........$24.99
00690608  Blue Wild Angel........$24.95
00275044  Both Sides of the Sky $22.99
00692932  Electric Ladyland.......$27.99
00690017  Live at Woodstock .....$29.99
00119619  People, Hell & Angels $24.99
00690602  Smash Hits ..............$24.99
00691152  West Coast Seattle
Boy (Anthology) ........$29.99
00691332  Winterland ..............$22.99

**H.I.M.**
00690843  Dark Light ...............$19.95

**Buddy Holly**
00660029  Best of ...................$22.99

**John Lee Hooker**
00690793  Anthology ................$29.99

**Howlin' Wolf**
00694905  Howlin' Wolf ............$22.99

**Billy Idol**
00690692  Very Best of.............$24.99

**Imagine Dragons**
00121961  Night Visions ..........$22.99

**Incubus**
00690688  A Crow Left of the
Murder....................$19.95

**Iron Maiden**
00690790  Anthology ................$24.99
00691058  The Final Frontier .....$22.99
00200446  Guitar Tab ...............$29.99
00690887  A Matter of Life
and Death ...............$24.95

**Alan Jackson**
00690730  Guitar Collection .......$29.99

**Elmore James**
00696938  Master of the
Electric Slide Guitar ..$19.99

**Jane's Addiction**
00690652  Best of....................$19.95

**Jethro Tull**
00690684  Aqualung.................$22.99
00690693  Guitar Anthology ......$24.99
00691182  Stand Up .................$22.99